THE COLOR GREEN

By Sarah Thomas

The lime is green.
1

The grape is green.

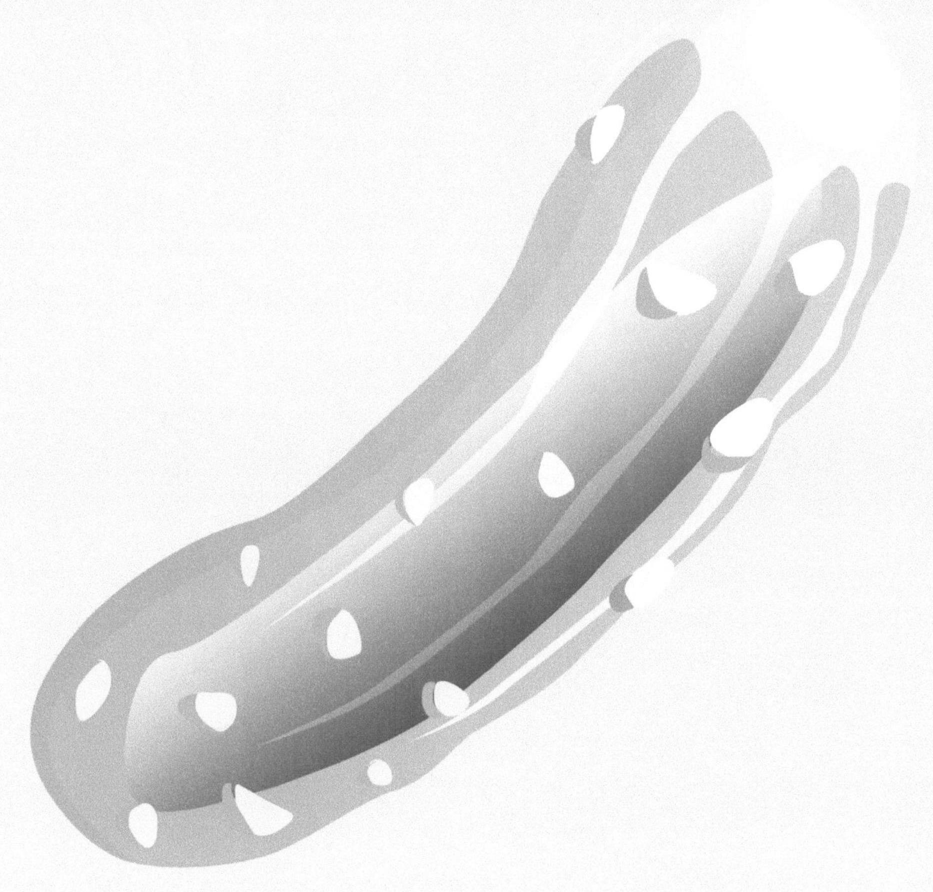

The pickle is green.

3

The tree is green.

4

The shirt is green.

The book is green.

The door is green.

The grass is green.

8

The grasshopper is green.

The frog is green.

The mug is green.

11

The broccoli is green.

12

The plant is green.

13

The chair is green.

14

The apple is green.

The coat is green.

16

The sucker is green.

The gummy bear is green.

18

The balloon is green.
19

The shoe is green.

The caterpillar is green.

The avocado is green.

The kiwi is green.

24

Learning to Read

Here are a few ideas to help your young reader.

1. Read to your child everyday.
2. Point to the words as you read.
3. Read the first two pages of the book and then have your child read the rest of the book.
4. Encourage your child to use the pictures to help them determine words.
5. As your child progresses in their reading abilities, encourage them to use the first letter of a word to determine what the word could be.